Care Bears™

PENGUIN BOOKS

PENGUIN BOOKS

UK | USA | Canada | Ireland | Australia | India | New Zealand | South Africa

Penguin Books is part of the Penguin Random House group of companies whose addresses can be found at global.penguinrandomhouse.com.

www.penguin.co.uk   www.puffin.co.uk   www.ladybird.co.uk

Penguin Random House UK

First published 2025
001

Copyright © 2025 Those Characters From Cleveland, LLC

Care Bears™ and related trademarks: TM & © 2025 Those Characters From Cleveland, LLC
Used under license by Penguin Books. Cloudco Entertainment with logo: TM & © 2025 Cloudco, LLC.
All rights reserved.

Penguin Random House values and supports copyright. Copyright fuels creativity, encourages diverse voices, promotes freedom of expression and supports a vibrant culture. Thank you for purchasing an authorized edition of this book and for respecting intellectual property laws by not reproducing, scanning or distributing any part of it by any means without permission. You are supporting authors and enabling Penguin Random House to continue to publish books for everyone. No part of this book may be used or reproduced in any manner for the purpose of training artificial intelligence technologies or systems. In accordance with Article 4(3) of the DSM Directive 2019/790, Penguin Random House expressly reserves this work from the text and data mining exception.

Printed in Slovakia

The authorized representative in the EEA is Penguin Random House Ireland,
Morrison Chambers, 32 Nassau Street, Dublin D02 YH68

A CIP catalogue record for this book is available from the British Library

ISBN: 978-0-241-80664-7

All correspondence to:
Ladybird Books, Penguin Random House Children's
One Embassy Gardens, 8 Viaduct Gardens, London SW11 7BW

FSC® C018179 — MIX Paper | Supporting responsible forestry

THE OFFICIAL COLOURING BOOK

PLACE A BLANK SHEET OF PAPER BEHIND THE PAGE IF USING WET PENS.

THIS BOOK BELONGS TO

. . . .

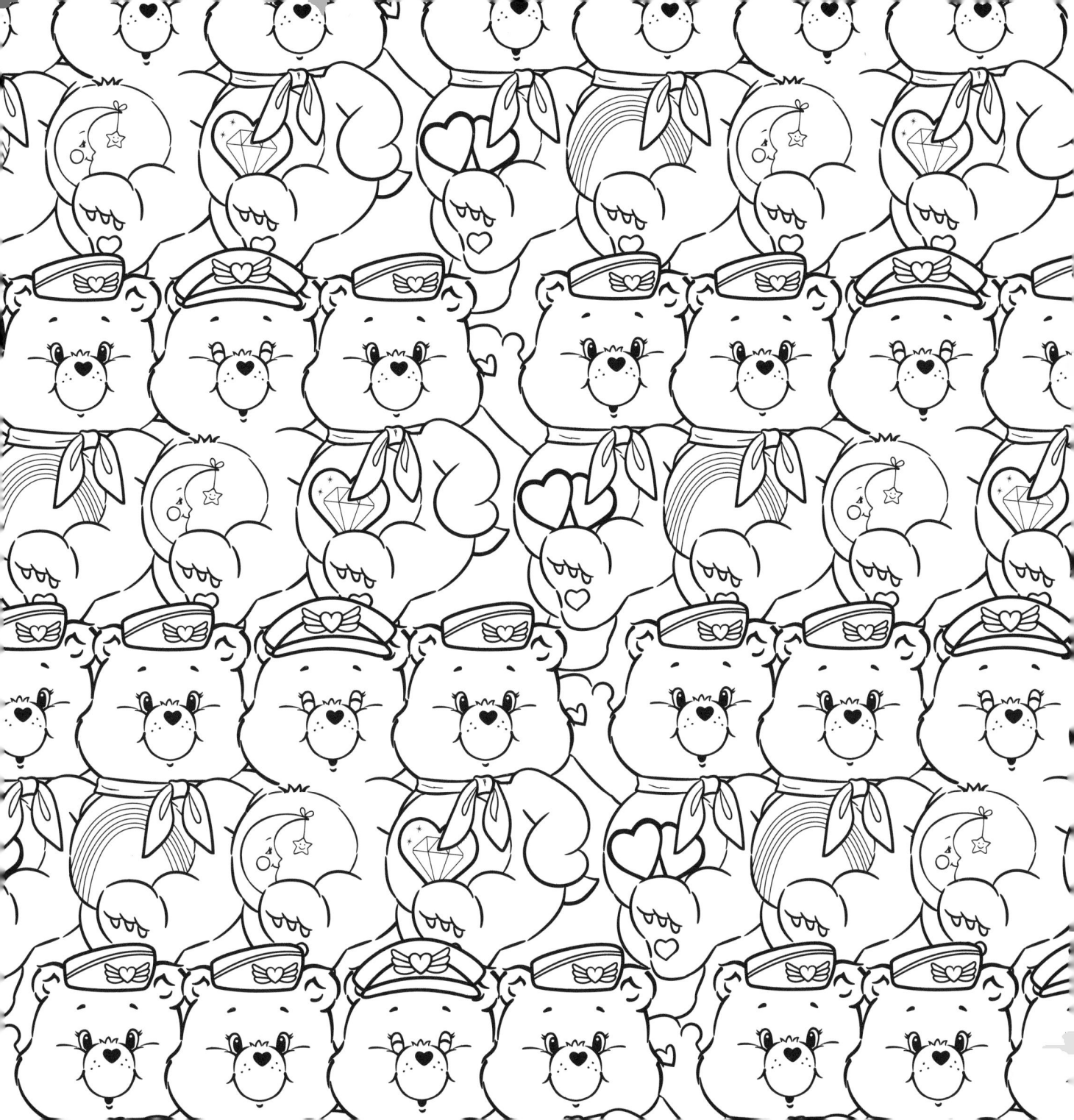